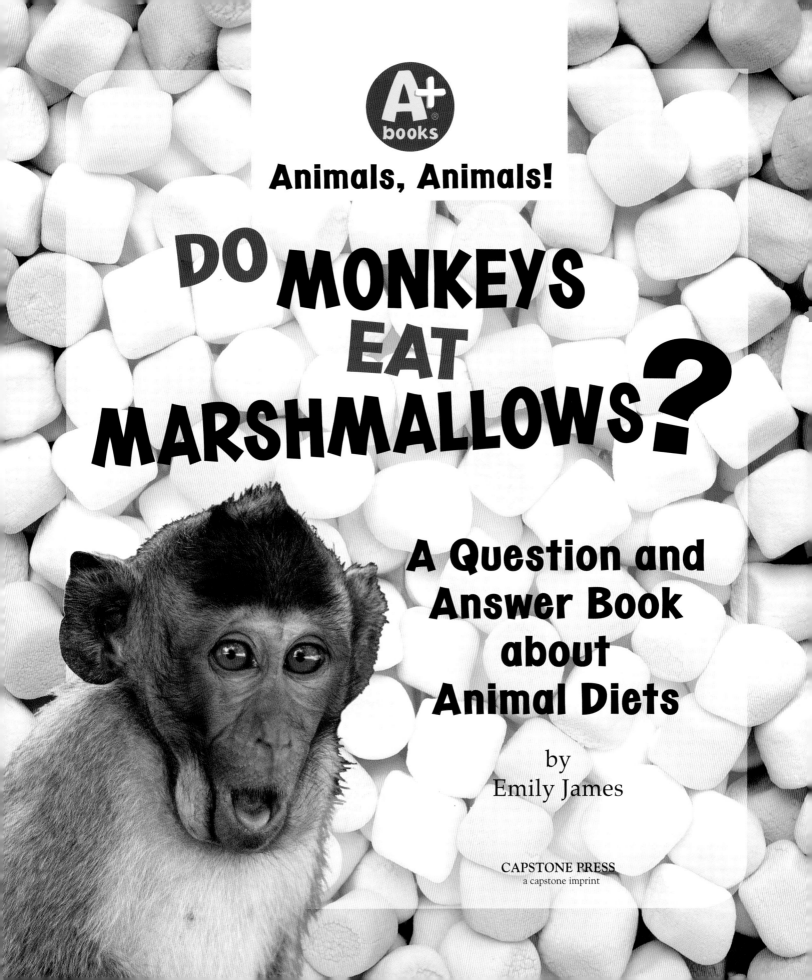

A+ books

Animals, Animals!

DO MONKEYS EAT MARSHMALLOWS?

A Question and Answer Book about Animal Diets

by
Emily James

CAPSTONE PRESS
a capstone imprint

A+ Books are published by Capstone Press,
1710 Roe Crest Drive, North Mankato, Minnesota 56003
www.mycapstone.com

Library of Congress Cataloging-in-Publication Data
Names: James, Emily, 1983–author.
Title: Do monkeys eat marshmallows? : a question and answer book about
   animals diets / by Emily James.
Description: North Mankato, Minnesota : Captstone Press, [2017] | Series: A+
   books. Animals, animals! | Audience: Ages 4-8. | Audience: K to grade 3.
   | Includes bibliographical references and index.
Identifiers: LCCN 2016005326 | ISBN 9781515726678 (library binding) | ISBN
   9781515726715 (paperback) | ISBN 9781515726753 (eBook PDF)
Subjects: LCSH: Animals–Food–Juvenile literature. | Animal
   behavior–Juvenile literature. | Children's questions and answers.
Classification: LCC QL756.5 .J36 2017 | DDC 591.5–dc23
LC record available at http://lccn.loc.gov/2016005326

EDITORIAL CREDITS:

Jaclyn Jaycox, editor; Juliette Peters, designer; Jo Miller, media researcher;
Laura Manthe, production specialist

IMAGE CREDITS:

iStockphoto: Peopleimages, 26; Minden Pictures: Katherine Feng, 22 (inset); Newscom: Arco Images G/picture alliance/Delpho, M., 20, 27 (top); Shutterstock: AngleArt, 24, Avirut Somsam, 12, belizar, 28 (top), Cloud7Days, cover (marshmallows), David Dirga, 4, David Ryo, 22, Ewais, 10, Ferderic B, 14, fontoknak, 1, back cover, Henk Paul, 28 (bottom), Jean-Edouard Rozey, 18, Karel Gallas, 16, Moize nicolas, 6, Naypong, 32, PyTy, 8, Ryan M. Bolton, cover (monkey), Volodymyr Goinyk, 27 (bottom)

DESIGN ELEMENTS:

Shutterstock: AN NGUYEN, djgis

NOTE TO PARENTS, TEACHERS, AND LIBRARIANS:

This Animals, Animals! book uses full-color images and a nonfiction format to introduce the concept of animal diets. *Do Monkeys Eat Marshmallows?* is designed to be read aloud to a pre-reader or to be read independently by an early reader. Images help listeners and early readers understand the text and concepts discussed. The book encourages further learning by including the following sections: Glossary, Critical Thinking Using the Common Core, Read More, Internet Sites, and Index. Early readers may need assistance using these features.

Printed in China.
007722

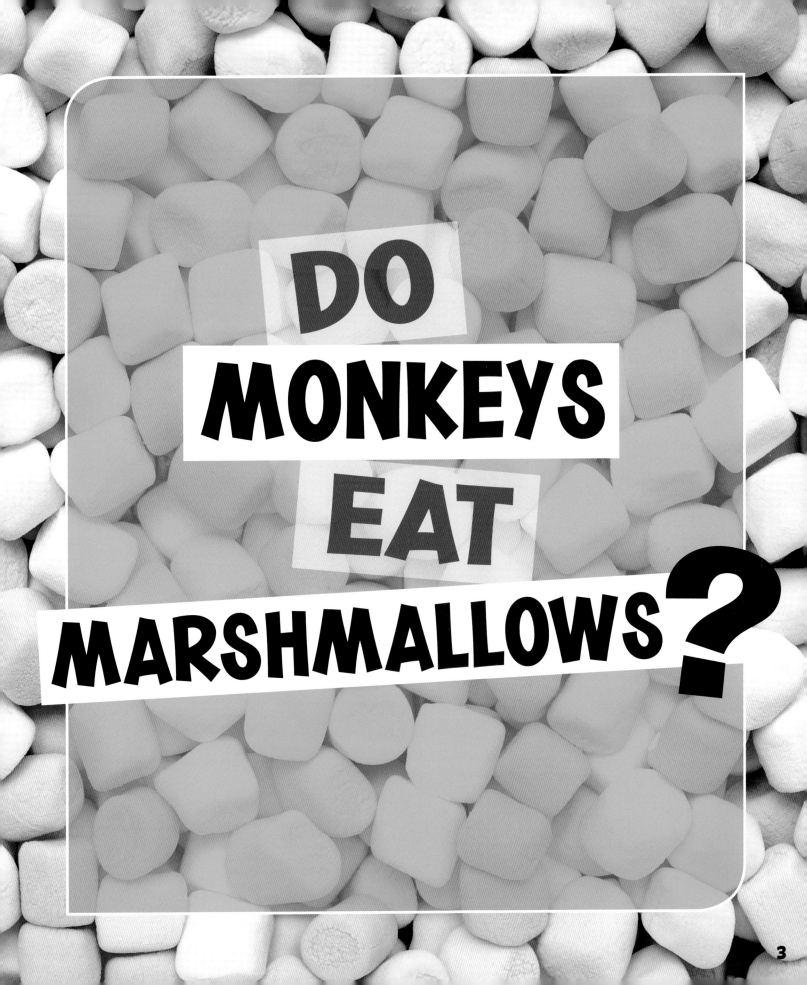

DO MONKEYS EAT MARSHMALLOWS?

No! Monkeys eat mangoes.

Monkeys scramble up fruit trees. They pluck sweet mangoes and tear them open. Monkeys also eat leaves and flowers. A frog, lizard, bat, or bug might even become a monkey's meal.

DO SHARKS EAT MARSHMALLOWS?

No! Sharks eat fish.

Sharks are giant ocean fish that eat smaller fish. Sharks have five to 15 rows of sharp teeth that can bite through bone.

DO GIRAFFES EAT MARSHMALLOWS?

No! Giraffes eat leaves.

Giraffes stretch their long necks to reach the branches of tall trees. They nibble at the leaves. A giraffe's tongue can slip between thorny branches. It can twist around a tasty bud.

DO COWS EAT MARSHMALLOWS?

No! Cows eat grass.

Cows graze on grass in green meadows. They also eat clover, peas, corn, and hay. Cows chew and swallow their food. They bring it up later to chew it some more. This is called cud.

DO RABBITS EAT MARSHMALLOWS?

No! Rabbits eat carrots.

Rabbits and bunnies eat carrots as a special treat. Wild rabbits eat mostly green, leafy plants. But in winter green leaves are scarce. Hungry rabbits eat twigs and tree bark.

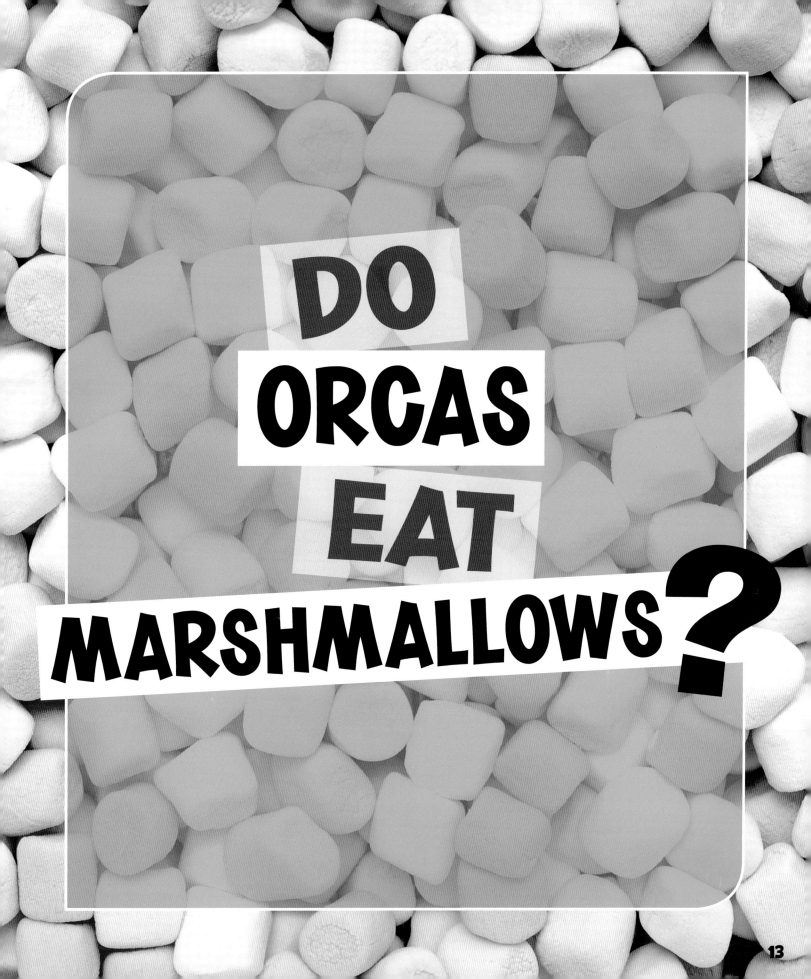

DO ORCAS EAT MARSHMALLOWS?

No! Orcas eat squid.

Orcas are good hunters. Besides squiggly squid, orcas eat fish, turtles, and seals. They even eat sea birds when they can catch them.

DO ANTEATERS EAT MARSHMALLOWS?

No! Anteaters eat ants.

Anteaters rip open anthills with their sharp claws. Their long, sticky tongues snatch up the scurrying ants. An anteater's tongue can worm its way deep into ant tunnels.

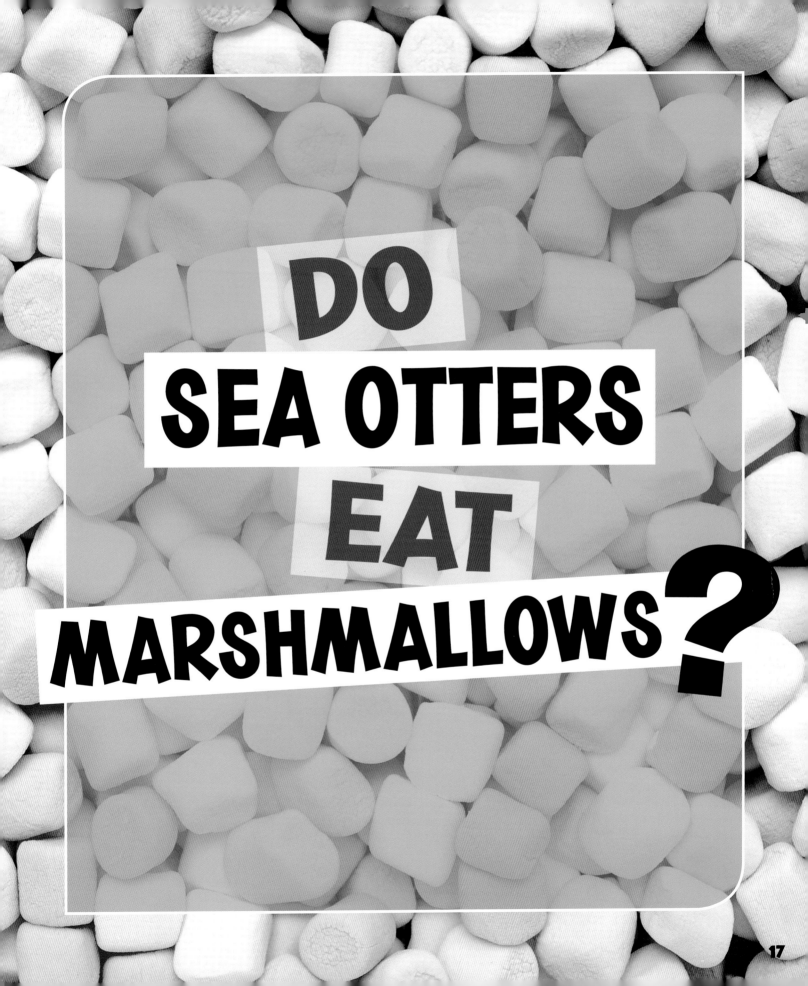

DO SEA OTTERS EAT MARSHMALLOWS?

No! Sea otters eat crabs.

Sea otters dive to the ocean floor to find food. They eat crabs, sea urchins, clams, fish, and snails. Sea otters bring their food to the water's surface. They eat while floating on their backs.

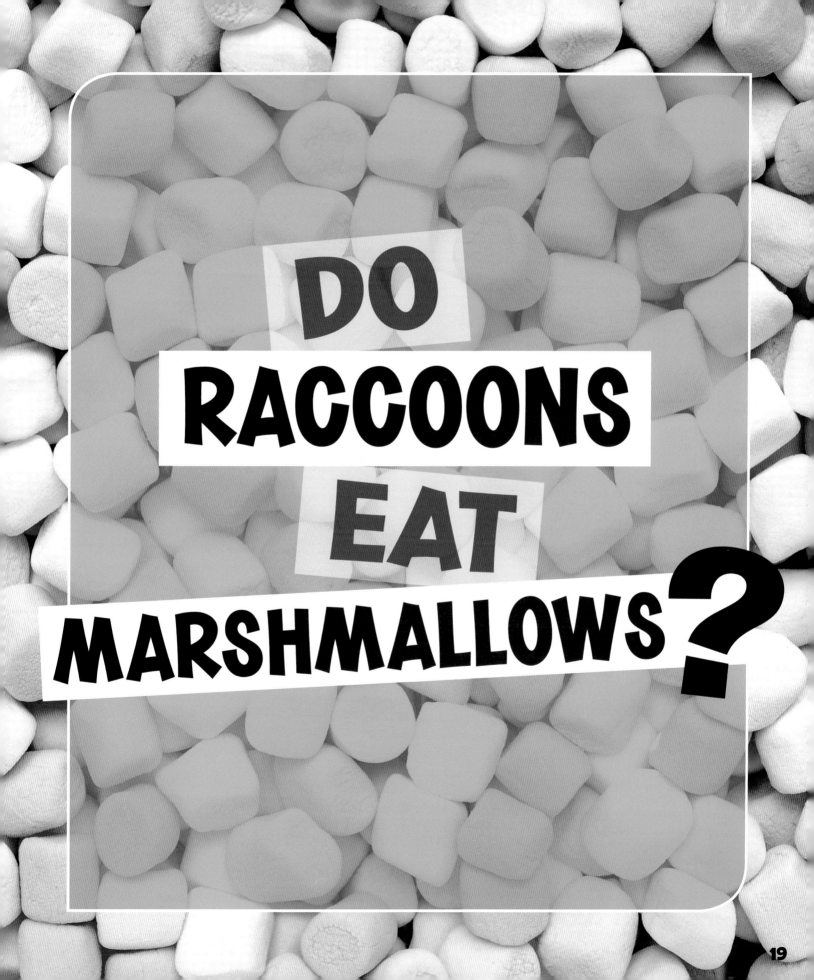

DO RACCOONS EAT MARSHMALLOWS?

No! Raccoons eat berries.

Raccoons ramble through bushes, picking berries with their paws. They also eat seeds, nuts, eggs, and fruit. Raccoons eat more food in fall to pack on extra fat for winter.

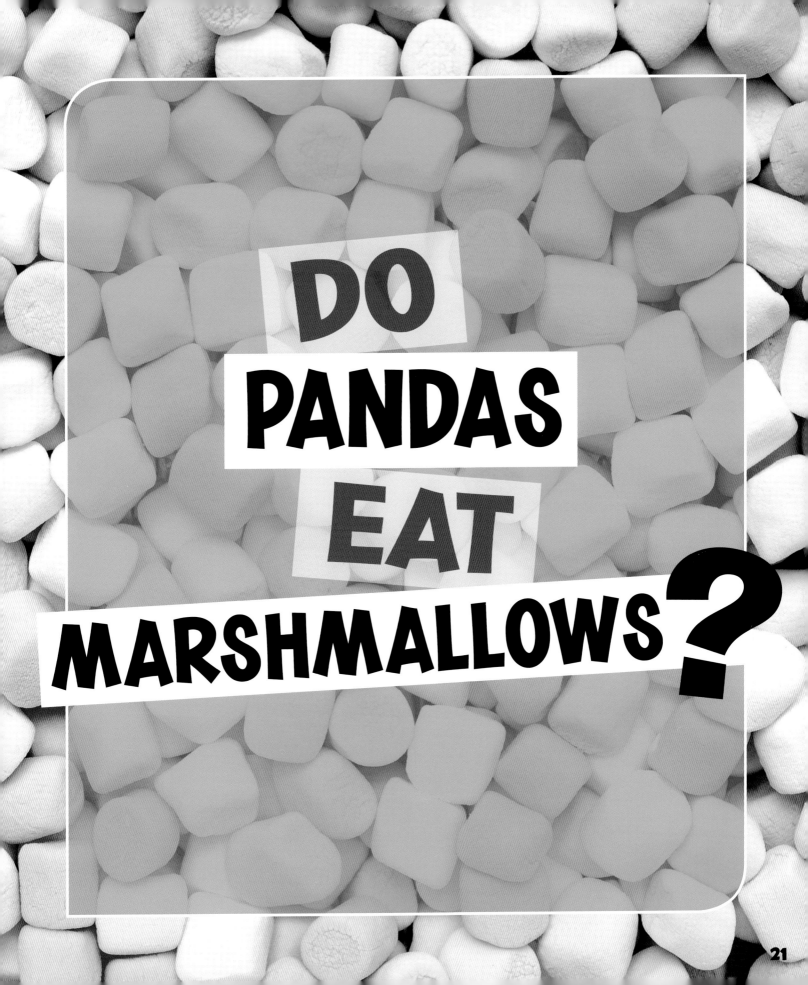

DO PANDAS EAT MARSHMALLOWS?

No! Pandas eat bamboo.

Pandas have special front paws with bony thumbs. The thumbs are good for gripping stiff bamboo stems. Powerful panda jaws and teeth chew through the stems and tough roots.

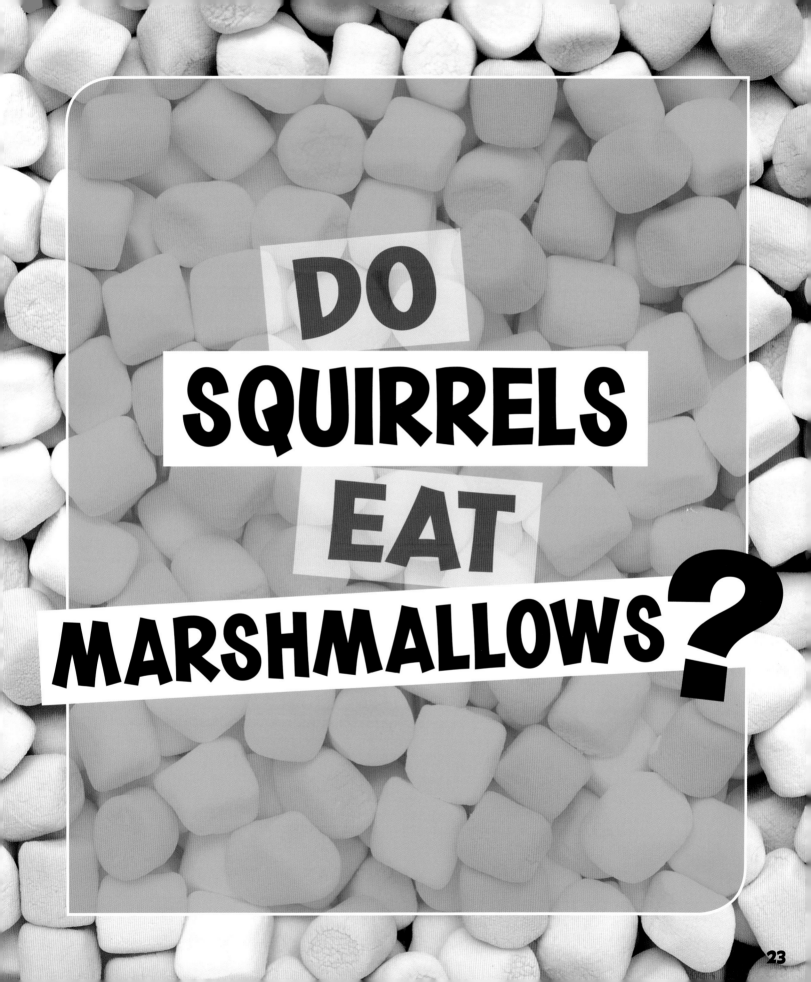

DO SQUIRRELS EAT MARSHMALLOWS?

No! Squirrels eat nuts.

Squirrels scamper through trees and leap from branch to branch. They search for food on the ground. Squirrels eat acorns, nuts, berries, and insects. They have sharp front teeth that never stop growing.

DO KIDS EAT MARSHMALLOWS?

Yes! Kids eat marshmallows.

Kids eat veggies and bread. They eat fruit and meat too. Kids eat lots of the same foods that animals eat. Kids eat food cooked on the stove or baked in the oven. For a special treat, kids might even eat marshmallows roasted over a fire!

Animal Diets

Animals eat soft things.

tangy berries ⟶ raccoons
squishy mangoes ⟶ monkeys
green grass ⟶ cows

Animals eat hard things.

chewy bamboo ⟶ pandas
crispy carrots ⟶ rabbits
crunchy nuts ⟶ squirrels

Raccoons love to eat berries.

a hungry panda eating bamboo

Animals eat things that wiggle and move.

slippery fish ⟶ sharks
squiggly squid ⟶ orcas
creepy-crawly ants → anteaters
snappy crabs ⟶ sea otters

an anteater searching for ants

a giraffe eating leaves

Animals eat food that grows up high.

tasty leaves on tall, tall trees ⟶ giraffes

GLOSSARY

anthill—a little hill of dirt made by ants when they dig their tunnels in the earth

bamboo—tall, stick-like plants with hard, hollow stems

bud—tightly closed flower or leaf that has not yet opened

clover—small, leafy plants that grow low to the ground

cud—partly chewed and swallowed food that a cow brings up again to chew some more

scarce—hard to find; leaves on trees are scarce during winter

sea urchin—a sea creature with a hard, spiny shell; the spines are used for protection and also help the sea urchin move around

squid—a sea animal with a long, soft body and 10 fingerlike arms used to grasp food

CRITICAL THINKING USING THE COMMON CORE

1. Which animal's front teeth never stop growing? (Key Ideas and Details)

2. Pandas use their strong jaws and teeth to chew bamboo. What is bamboo? (Craft and Structure)

3. What kinds of food does your favorite animal eat? (Integration of Knowledge and Ideas)

READ MORE

Benefield, James. *Herbivores*. What Animals Eat. Chicago: Heinemann Library, 2015.

Kalman, Bobbie. *How and What Do Animals Eat?* All About Animals Close-Up. New York: Crabtree Publishing Company, 2015.

Kalman, Bobbie. *Rapping About What Animals Eat*. Rapping About. New York: Crabtree Publishing Company, 2012.

INTERNET SITES

FactHound offers a safe, fun way to find Internet sites related to this book. All of the sites on FactHound have been researched by our staff.

Here's all you do:

Visit *www.facthound.com*

Type in this code: 9781515726678

 Check out projects, games and lots more at **www.capstonekids.com**

LOOK FOR ALL THE BOOKS IN THE SERIES

DO COWS HAVE KITTENS?
A Question and Answer Book about Animal Babies

DO GOLDFISH FLY?
A Question and Answer Book about Animal Movements

DO MONKEYS EAT MARSHMALLOWS?
A Question and Answer Book about Animal Diets

DO WHALES HAVE WHISKERS?
A Question and Answer Book about Animal Body Parts

INDEX